Scratching Initials

by
Linda Pearce

Bracken Books
BC Canada

for my sister

Phyllida Pearce.

CONTENTS

Introduction

Several years ago when my mother died, I found among her belongings one of my sister's childhood novels, *What Katy Did Next,* by Susan Coolidge. I was touched to see her name, Phyllida Pearce, written on the flyleaf in her childish hand.

Phyl, suffered from what I've now come to believe were absence seizures, small epileptic seizures, which caused her to lead a life interrupted by constant breaks in consciousness. When she was sixteen she had her first of many grand mal seizures and when she was twenty five she suffocated in her pillow while locked in the grip of another. The memories of her difficult life and early death are painful, and although I have tried to write about her, I have never found a way in.

After wondering what to do with the book for awhile, I finally decided to use the vocabulary from a single page to inspire a poem, as a way of reaching back to connect her with my present life. I would start the process by making a word bank from the page, and then allow the words to interlace with something in the day or in my imagination at the time, which would lead me into a poem. I have called it *Scratching Initials* because of the indelible marks her short presence made on me, and also because I have put my own initials on words she enjoyed during her life.
As a result the poems are eclectic in subject and form, bound together only by the thread of their common inception.

FOOD FOR THE AGES

the teeth of her babies,
hung around her neck
like a string of dull pearls.
milk dribbled from her breasts,
tributaries over ranges
that puddled between her toes.
her gut rippled with crying,
saline dripped from her chin
her hands wrung themselves
over and over in snake knots.

They're dead, she said,
All taken,
no headstones,
so hard.
why couldn't they leave me
just one?

Vermin gathered — rats and mice,
creeping to devour the milk,
greedy ant swarms
claimed their share.
song birds supped her tears
and made nests in her hair,
their feces dropped seeds,
which sprouted in her
valleys and crevices,
trees took root,
blossoms fed butterflies and bees,
finally, the scavengers came,
crows, ravens,
vultures eager for carrion,
a curtain of shadows
spreading her flesh in the four directions.
worms took the final nourishment.

her bones though, they're still there
rattling with sobs
beneath the pavement.

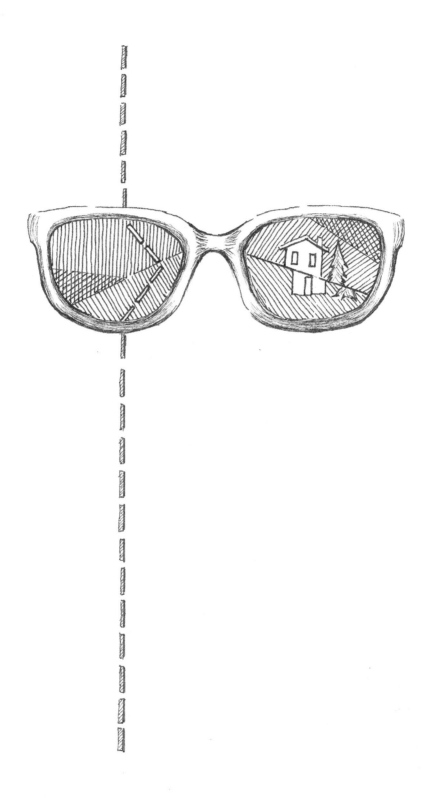

WHERE ARE THE BOUNDARIES

The borders wag and wibble,
their lines are indistinct,
my glasses are not well made,
the filters are faulty
and molded by shoddy crafters,
on battered equipment,
salvaged from the rubbish
of those at ease with their
needle point vision.
I stumble into ravines
and rush headlong into bogs.
try to replace the lenses,
buy new ones from a shiny shop,
where other people have accounts
You need a prescription,
the clerks look with confusion
when asked where to find an optometrist,
as if I were asking how to breathe,
just in and out, it's obvious.
wire and glue, I make my own
cobble together bits left in coffee shops
or in the waiting rooms of doctors
sometimes, the combination
works for a while
and hazards stand out
clear, precise.
I puff with confidence.
until I forget them in the library,
or drop them while
running for the bus.
in time I've found one fairly good lens
with only a smudge at the edge
and one with a few streaks and scratches
that work if I tilt my head
and look at an angle
out of the corner of my eye.

PUPPET MASTERS

We make effigies of ourselves,
with shiny scraps and bits
from trunks and chests,
stored in dusty
chambers of our hearts.
We send them holding hands
to live our lost lives,
feed them our yearnings,
point directions
to tender-heart wishes
and stories altered
to snugly fit our dream.

They live out perfection,
in sun slanted forests,
barefoot on beaches,
naked in lakes,
flying with eagles
through cracks in the sunset,
they tune up their voices
to sing the old songs,
warming their feet
in vats of wild honey,
rolling in blossoms,
at rest in goose down.

In the cold of the dawn
they melt at our feet
we label containers
and stuff them back in.

We are puppet masters
our program is written,
ink's dry on the contract,
the show must go on.

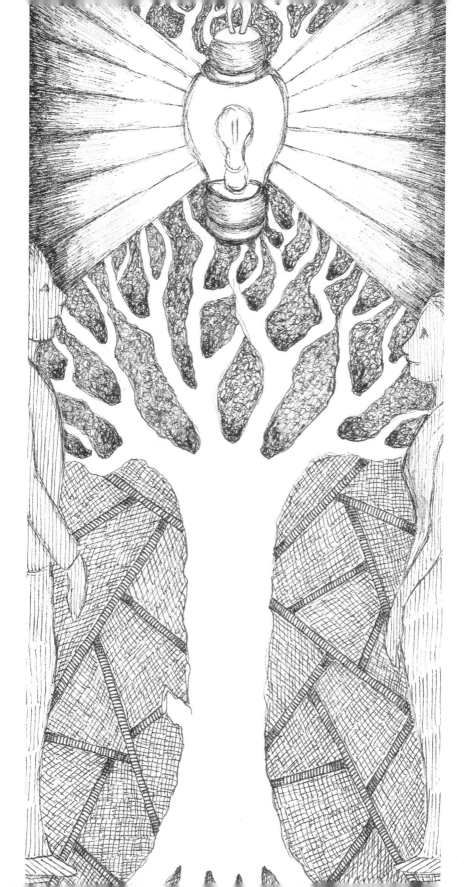

I KNOW YOU'RE OUT THERE — SOMEWHERE

Through kindred cells, I feel your echo lamp,
in lucid pools of friends I most admire.
In glints of yellow leaves that light a fire
and blaze a swath, across the many damp
twig trails I hoped would lead me to your camp.
On days when loneliness infests desire
and sculpts the clay of fear to tightened wire,
which cuts and scars the body like a stamp,
I've stood knee deep on decks of sinking ships,
reached my hand for lifeboats made of straw,
that sink like stones inside a cotton sack.
The pressure of a thousand tiny drips
has drained my half full cup and left me raw,
remembering the camel's broken back.

Remembering the camel's broken back,
I've surrendered mendicant and my tin bowl,
to blueprint channels, circling the shoal
of quicksand. In my boots and heavy pack
I bargain for new rules, that bend the track
toward the bridge and street where you pay toll.
My wearing frictions leave a gaping hole,
familiar, vacant and swept clear of flack.
Artists offer brushstrokes of good grace,
you would love the colour and their style
of piling paint, and you would love the font
the writers use, for words that won't erase
from such a soft and tender surface, while
the earth turns on a prism point of want.

The earth turns on a prism point of want,
a rainbow join, although we've never met
the knowing hovers, dense like unpaid debt.
Morse footsteps send out messages to haunt
corridors of sculpture, where thoughts will taunt
the weathered shammy of our ease, and fret
wreathing poultice pulls inside the chest, yet
release the disbelief that draws a gaunt
and empty avatar. Preconception
holds a pulpit, which never feeds us back.
Just face into the hurricane, and tramp
pathways that are close, resist deception
or magic, know by everything you hack,
through kindred cells, I feel your echo lamp.

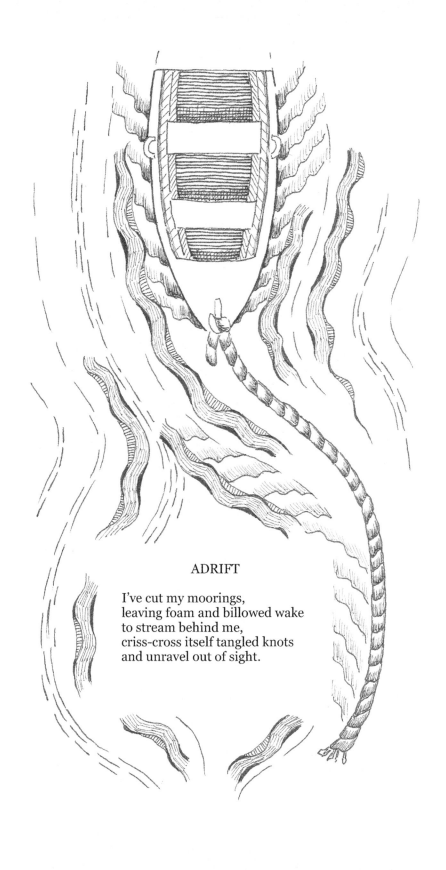

ADRIFT

I've cut my moorings,
leaving foam and billowed wake
to stream behind me,
criss-cross itself tangled knots
and unravel out of sight.

PARAMETERS

Such a narrow path

I thought it would squeeze out life

restrict creations

but it funnelled intentions

into stronger brighter blooms.

BELLS OF GRIEF

When the messenger comes, we shut the door — lock and bolt — sever the connecting thread. Then pull the page back, suffocate veracity's bird until it's struggling wings lie still. We'll tear up the letters, telegrams, cut the phone line, scramble the wi fi, shoot the pigeons as they try to land. The tidings are not glad, are unwanted. Their rolling pages batter the pilings.

We'll curl around our fat lizard, protect it from whispers loud as thunder, explosive cocktails, rapid fire that vibrates through the floor, through fingers, through ear plugs, through blankets. If necessary we must scream, stamp, beat the walls, lower the sky with it's thick clouds, pull down the night blanket and shades of weary mesh.

Remember not to clean the windows, or accept bids to clear stacks of broken furniture, barricaded against exits. There is no bright adventure, bells of grief ring spells of silence, clogged with unlived moments. At all costs, delay the unread story.

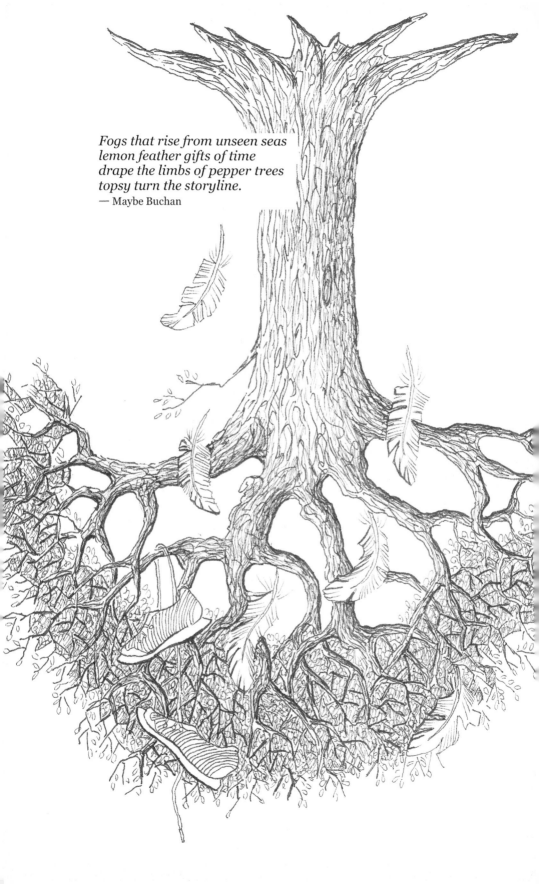

*Fogs that rise from unseen seas
lemon feather gifts of time
drape the limbs of pepper trees
topsy turn the storyline.*
— Maybe Buchan

REGRET

She wishes she had
floated downstream,
across trout water paths,
clumps of frog spawn
and through tree arches,
clasping knotted fingers,
the white water coaster
spraying jewel tips on her hair,
her vision straining through misted
fogs that rise from unseen seas.

She wishes she had
risen before the dew,
walked barefoot
toward the woods,
where the bird last nested
content in spring leaves,
it's voice a croon of soft notes
taking captives, the preen
of it's beak scattering light
lemon feather gifts of time.

She wished she had
taken pictures of their faces,
maybe then she'd remember
something other than
trudging bundles, eyes of shadows,
children dragged by arms,
bare feet off the ground,
belongings dropped or cast off,
left to clutter the roadside, or
drape the limbs of pepper trees.

She wished she had
taken the cliff path to the shore,
where she could wash her eyes
and ears with the sweet ocean,
sieve from the sand of her mind
poisonous memory.
The glutted sea air
gifts it's excess freely
nourishing all wishes to
topsy turn the story the line.

SUMMER OF FIRES

These ransacked days
of heat and smoke,
red ball glow,
I am on fire,
burning,
my body vibrates,
hot rubber legs,
wobble and sink.
flames rise through my torso
melting arms, shoulders, fingertips.

a charred wind plays across blue velvet,
billows over the raised faces of dahlias,
humming birds lost in the grey,
starve within inches of nectar,
bees bumble into corners.

Face north to the dragons,
miles and miles of them — legions,
their toes spread, scales lifted
and furnace breath
spewing cauterized caresses
great wings hooding
across treetops like
cloud shadows.
contemporary divinities
claws embedded
in a heathen grip
know how to sacrifice,
negotiate with gods,
a beetle for a butterfly.

And my sweet breath
diluted by smog
streams over charred twigs
and burnt bridges.
the children inside us lock arms,
stamp through ashes
that rise like chimney smoke,
to meet flames lighting the tips of our hair.

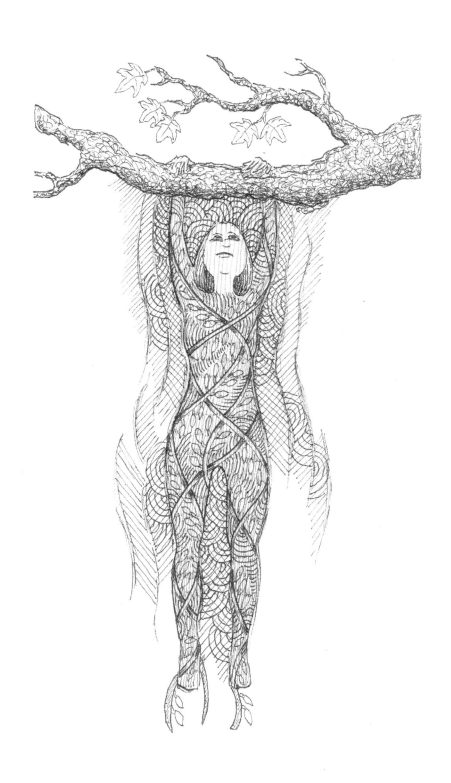

LOOSENING BARK

She hangs from the branch like a vine from the wrist
of a statue. Her fingers dig into the loosening bark.
The groves are deep. It is a seasoned tree, like the old
growth she locked arms on picket lines to protect. A
beetle crawls across her thumb. A breeze sends the
canopy waving, twigs clack together like rhythm
sticks. Higher up, a pileated woodpecker drills its
beak into the trunk and a squirrel finds a crevice
where an acorn is hidden.
— Then she lets go.

I wish I could fly.
wing tips combing dew from clouds,
breast into updraft,
watching life's jumbled threads,
loosen, unwind and weave smooth.

It is estimated that sixty tons of cosmic dust land on the earth each day.

COSMIC DUST

I feel the weight of it,
the cosmic dust,
making earth heavier,
becoming part of ourselves,
stardust that we breathe and eat
sliding through bloodstreams,
tiny ambassadors
from the vast unknown,
entering our brains,
vibrations turning thoughts
to align with some obscure,
unmapped plan.
does it guide my fingers
to write these words,
remind me
I am not in control,
but that millions of
undeclared intentions
bargain for the fruit
of every moment,
shooting from all directions
flight paths
kept from collision
by the artistic direction
of some great astral conductor.

THE FOX

By the Yukon river on a bright morning, a red fox
stepped across the path. It was young, pristine, an
idealized picture from a wildlife magazine. No
mangy patches or battle scars. The tail floated,
responsive, like a wind sleeve.
Our eyes locked and held, paws whispered
forward. Limbs fluid as stretched dough, hovered,
barely touching the ground. Sun-streaks dappled
by birch stems, rippled red, gold, red, gold, across
orange fur, to touch charged whiskers, probing
like caterpillars on a leaf.
Twin snapped — gone

A distilled moment,
extends to eternity,
holds us immortal,
as the breath of a small fox,
may reach to the firmament.

BARE BULB

Stains scamper across flocked wallpaper and mold crawls out from torn patches. A crucifix left by an earlier tenant, hangs above the metallic rungs of the bed. Drooping at its edges, the chenille spread is balding along one side. Fug of last week's onions, high pitched scrape of chairs upstairs. A rust stained sink with the cold tap dripping in four-four time, stands against one wall and a bare bulb hangs from the ceiling. It looks for all the world, like the set from and old 1950s film about a nicotined private eye. But it is not, it is where he lives, his home. Unmoved by luxury or visual aesthetics, his joy comes from the wall of dog eared books, the huge battered desk with one leg propped on an ancient catalogue, and papers holding hands across its surface.

It takes so little,
to unwrap the stone of truth
and fully satisfy life.

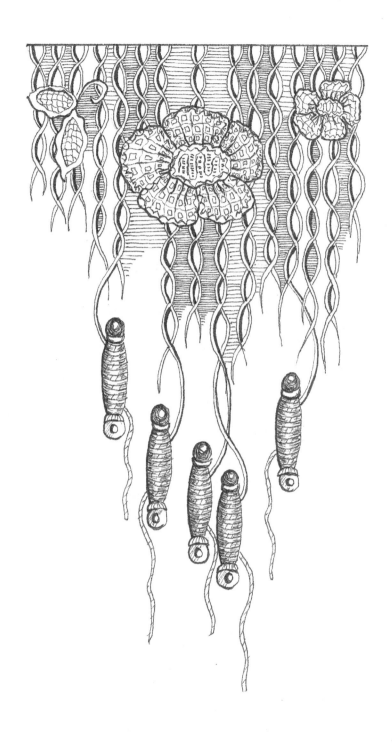

THE LACEMAKER

I saw her three times,
The Lacemaker,
We sat together,
a quiet young woman,
intent on her craft,
subdued light glazing her head.
I showed her my new scarf.

To the left, a room
filled with twelve foot Rubens,
bulky languid nudes,
floor to gold leaf ceiling.

And yet she holds her place,
her tiny square of wall,
one pixel in the massive image
of the Louvre's interior,
content in 17th century
thoughts and concerns.
I asked her how she
handled loneliness.
She had no wisdom
on the subject,
but silently offered
a portal of insulation
from huddled tour groups
and travellers lining up selfies.

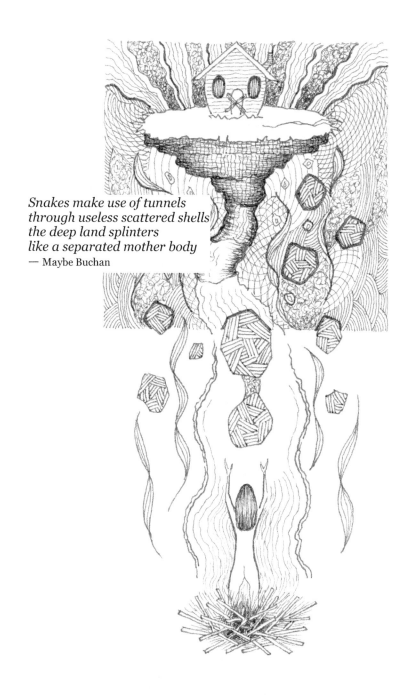

Snakes make use of tunnels
through useless scattered shells
the deep land splinters
like a separated mother body
— Maybe Buchan

PAY YOUR WAY

Never go back to once was home,
find a moment, recall a dawn,
or dig through silt and heavy mud
sieve the muck and mire of guilt,
or wish to find a glimmer house
through sorcery of time,
hoping for a glimpse of light
or a tunnel, but then, only
snakes make use of tunnels.

Never go back to once was home
across loose shale that slides away,
rolling agates bounce the slope.
bury deep your crystal truth,
carried back in weary arms.
delusion fills your empty cup
the age you cling to will be dust
you'll only wade in sift soft sand
through useless scattered shells.

Never go back to once was home
to find a better story.
The ground is now unstable.
Fissures frame and fracture.
The shake of crumbled bedrock
will never give you peace, but
throw your need in twisted mass
to thrash face down, while
the deep land splinters.

Never go back to once was home.
The door is sealed and windows locked.
Fill your lungs with clearer air,
hold the place you've newly built,
a soft and downy comfort nest,
with kindness and the smell of earth.
Pay your way with memory
floating on the wind
like a separated mother body

PRINTMAKERS

Impressions are left in the mud, heavy footprints and lighter, smaller ones beside. I note the outer heel on the larger prints worn down, and the clear even tread in the lighter steps. Not the thoughts though — not the hearts and souls or circumstances of the printmakers. Whether they go home to a mansion or cardboard box under the overpass, or if they are mourning a mother, worried about cancer or going blind. Is it college fees or the next meal that keep them up at night. A Nobel laureate may be walking with their son, celebrating the prize, or an addict with their partner celebrating one week sober.
I follow them to the edge of the pond.

There is no escape,
whether we sing high or low,
human nature draws
melodies from the same notes
and repertoire of rhythms

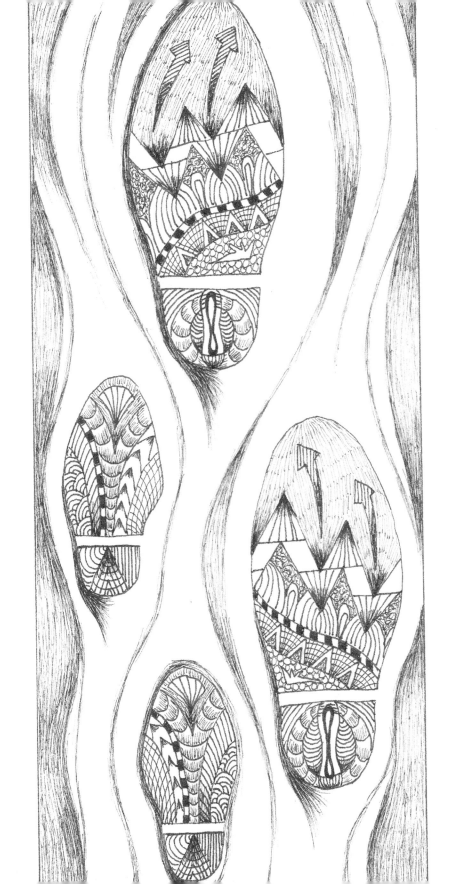

WHY DO PEOPLE EVER GO TO SEA? It's like a call, they say, a summons to sail out over that great green unstable vastness. Ride the rollers like watery mountains, up and down, tilting the horizon.

The horizon, my guide my constant, the caress of earth and sky. I spill coffee over nautical maps and my fingers cling to the railing like crab claws. My steely eyeballs swivel down toward dark fathoms, thick, translucent and so very, very deep. The welter of water works a hypnotic suction, a beckoning lap and swirl. Ribbons of foam reach up to knot around my limbs.

A tide of memory sweeps backward, fidget spins mind corners and teases a kernel of amphibious knowing, shared by millennia of great greats, before the crawling gasp for air. A tiny synapsis still firing, whispers of the weightless ease of an elastic spine, harmonized to ebb and flow, the thrum and pulse of fin and tail, ease of swim, float, glide, in and out of gills, vision blurred through a liquid prism, the mossy taste of algae and the wa wa beat against the drums of my ears.

INTO THE WOODS

Step into shadowfall,
hold it's cool gloaming,
against the thin skin
of your tenderized heart.
like the dance of a sea mist
in treetops bent windward
and cedar scent sun-streaks
on trillium blooms.

Breath becomes
an inhale of patience,
plastic exits through pores
opened to smells
of needles and sleeping buds.
trunks pour like monk's robes
to puddle on the ground.
tangled moss beards,
drift across lullabies
of jade and chartreuse.
brown and brittle arms
reach up like antennae to the gods,
they do not seek or journey,
prattle or demand rights,
but rest obedient,
accepting buffets,
forgiving our unkindness,
our toxic rains and axes,
branch tents of protection,
over moist matted mulch,
incubating new guardians,
— nourishing
in protoplasmic segments.
archivists of an alternate
unspoke history.

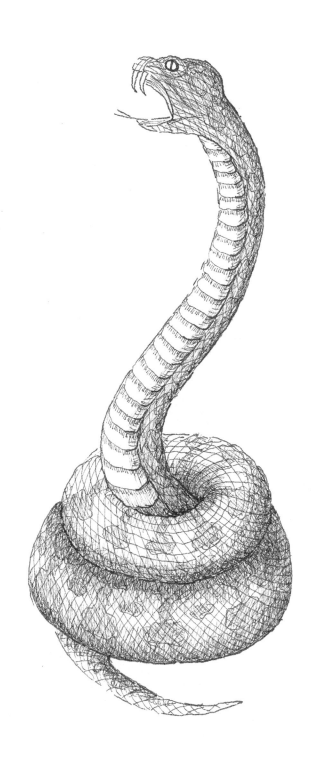

HINGED TONGUES

Sliding through fine filters
there is nothing of tolerance
in their announcements,
nothing of mercy
in their words,
only a coiled viper,
mouth agape and frozen
like a tarnished statue.

they can advertise,
they can speak of intention,
babble assurances,
apologies,
the air has curdled,
there is no pardon,
while their breath
evaporates all regret
and the angels of honesty
asphyxiate
in the laden fumes.

the door is marked,
the sword unsheathed,
letters are extruded into
unrecognizable shapes,
meaning wrung from madness,
speak out cowed millions,
hold your shrinking thought
before the moment
melts in your palm.

there is a rising,
a community of lovers,
stand dear comrades,
against the weasel words
that wind and whip,
unravel them
with bloody fingers
catch them as
they slither, jump, fly
and burrow underground.

BUBBLES OF ORDINARY

I swallowed a hole,
it rests beside my heart,
I feed it ripened mango,
pools of maple syrup,
there is a drain, a straw
that sucks the fruity syrup,
invites black pudding
coated in gravel,
ready with rubbing salt.

it draws an acid mist
and the claws of owls,
at times white rice
or simmered oatmeal
bland, nutritious, steady.
I block the drain
with bluebird's wings,
pump in helium,
and chocolate mousse.

the relentless hollow
stalks my thoughts,
refusing delicate pastries,
notes in perfect harmony,
wildflowers in alpine meadows.
it hums in my chest,
a jackhammer of energy,
wringing and squeezing out
bubbles of ordinary.

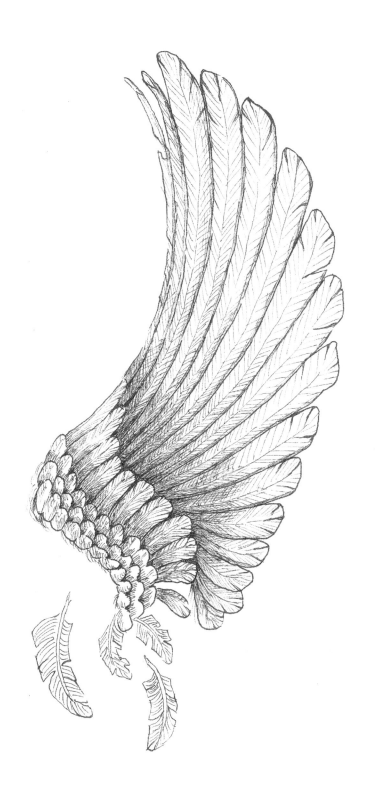

THE WAY OF THE LYNX

From their seats around the bonfire they see a lynx in the bushes, eyes lit by the flames — flickering. The minute becomes smug with itself. On a parallel plane, pop-culture sages set up correspondence. Emails are written, stories sent out, pictures uploaded, tweets dancing across timelines repeat phrases into concrete. Meetings organize focus groups, pursue lines of inquiry, channels are kept open and the envelope pushed. The video goes viral.
— The bushes rustle, the flicker moves away and a marshmallow drops from its stick into the embers. Hsss!

All their sad stories,
melted into the darkness
like ice on a grill

KOKO EXPRESS — PORTRAITS

The three faces hang,
men — black and white,
photographs, black and white,
civil rights, entitled whites,
suspended on a rust wall.
sun streaking across the glass,
reflects the orange lights along
the barista bar.

old men, faces scripted,
pregnant with story.
streams of days past,
crawl through beard forests
and hang in looping neck skin,

fat cheek pouches reminisce
smiles at new babies
and family "in" jokes,
eyes like wells, remember
falling in love with
a young woman on the bus,
the affair with a cousin's wife.
a Grizzly encounter,
on the west coast trail,
the song Dad hummed
while he fixed the car,
a medal earned for saving a child,
a biological mother met late
and held tight.
childhood trauma, hard labour,
the goodness of the neighbours
when the house burned down.

shiny pates cradle
accomplishments,
pinched from calendar clay,
once they knew everything,
now nothing,
black and white
battered like tanned leather
into infinite shades of grey.

TAKE ME HOME

Leaf boats sail full canvas
into bramble edged woods,
tree arches rise
and vanish in the mist
rejoice if you can,
celebrate the the green womb,
exclaim in delight
if that is your nature,
there is no shame in joy,
no hypocrisy in rousing cheers.

After all,
acrobats are paid
to walk thin lines,
balance on knife edges,
these things are not
for the unskilled.
yet, they shudder to glimpse
through grey gloom,
bleached white rope
and plastic islands,
against the wild breezes
and polluted seas,
where seven eyed fish
glide without direction,
sightless in a rancid soup.

Do not leave me in these ruins,
shot through the heart,
abandoned like a horseman
frozen in summer fields,
where mice gather grains
around his feet and
make nests with bits of straw.

Take me home
where fresh winds
smell of salt and seaweed,
trees stoop along the cliffs
and eagles spread and float.

Stop the tides that whisper secrets
keep the secrets of whispering tides.

TOO EASY

Dozens of roads branch out like spiders legs, but only one glows. That's the one she follows. Placing her feet carefully, she feels a slight hum rising through her soles, which enlivens her body. The trees in the distance are backlit with an ethereal aura and the one tall building visible, blinks its window eyes, rolling out its steps like a ridged tongue.
Something turns red in her gut. She swivels, hurries back to the intersection and steps out in a rough brown direction, a gravel trail with scattered rocks and fisted roots.

Where is the challenge
in paths slippery as silk,
the air like sugar
syrup melting in the lungs
too sweet, too smooth, too easy.

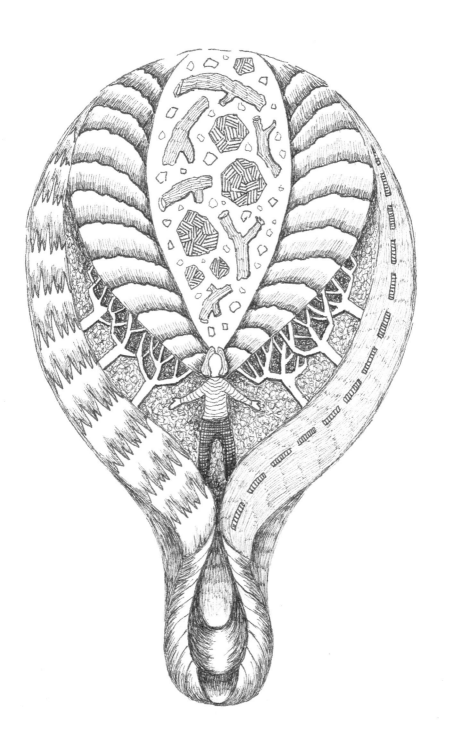

MICRO PARIS

Travelling alone in micro Paris,
micro London, Prague, Rome
in cold soda terror,
scabbed warriors
rein in successive battalions,
across boardwalks dry with rot
and colonies of carpenter ants.
no one greets their bulging guts,
or runs fingers through their matted hair
with gentle humanity.
no butterflies light on their padded shoulders,
or birdsongs brush their stiff cheeks.
crumbling planks form dusty holes
shaped in their images,
they slide into a slow motion free-fall,
saved by a mesh of electronic waves,
beating 'round their heads
in blind confusion
like crazed bats,
cocooned, shaped,
projected on screens
they live.

powerless mothers weep
and lay flowers,
their sorrow so discreet,
eleven times returning
to the place where they feel known,
where voices speak their language
a language lost in micro Paris.

REMEMBERING GWAII

Mind crossings mired in misty perma-bog
draw trails of moss through our colonial doubt
while scattered treebones brace a surf scoured log
painstaking footprints never do wash out.
Our blowhole fancies edge the foldstone rim,
contrived and steeping in a clubstump swelled
by endless sand and waving beach grass whim.
We cannot claim the unknown that's been felled,
soft clamshell bodies, built with agate hands
and washed with kelp frond fingers by the shore.
A kindly windwitch weaves through Sitka stands
and slips a stitch through every living pore.
Tap wisdom roots that hold the line each day,
inflate earths gasping lungs in lands away.

I KNOW YOUR NATURE

Nobody notices scuffed shoes
polished with spit,
brushed hair
pulled free of twigs,
or the carefully chosen dress,
with only two buttons missing,
nobody notices her battered bonnet
bent up on one side,
invisible, her breath
joins the crowds of
sidewalk bumpers,
in and out,
shaping the air.

I love you,
caress you with my mind,
lay my affection on the pavement
to rise through your feet,
expose my living insides
to your abrasion.
I know your nature,
we walk together in imagination,
beyond fatigue
beyond the fraying patchwork,
clipped and stapled
into amorphous shapes,
straggly, piecemeal lives,
brewed together in a rich sauce.

Their steps lighten
to the melodies of
bright new songs.
the air sweetens,
crisp as fresh lettuce,
hearts escape chests,
arteries knotting together
in communion.
she sits on the bus stop bench,
folds her hands and smiles.
I am a witch.

SHUT THE DOOR

Not this day
tasks that test metal,
or wield the knife of truth
in a slice to the bone.

Shut the door,
spread a downy surface
fringed with ermine,
soft lace made by nuns in retreat,
bumps and lumps ironed out,
rough places sanded,
nothing to cause tossing, distress
or a change in position.
velvet oceans wave lightly
as a vapour cloud,
warm as a polar coat,
draughts plugged and sealed,
panpipe notes step like fairies
into dusted ears
half plugged with cotton,
colours hold hands in solidarity
with tertiary ease,
lavender and Lily
ply scents that woo
nothing left to moulder,
decompose or wilt,
only surfaces scrubbed
with sanitary wipes.
no love, not anger
jealousy, compassion,
no broken hearts
no failures
no life
and no death allowed in here.

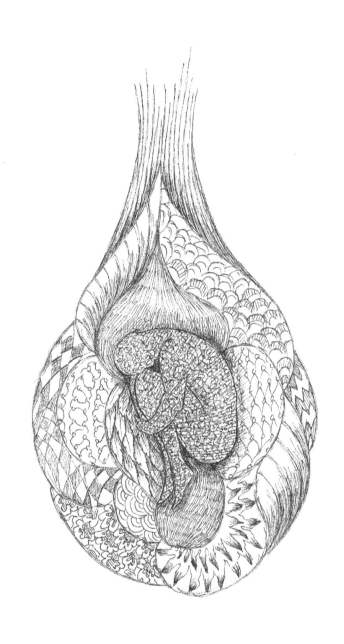

buckets brought to gather plunder
on a steamship of fat chance
warn the youth of salt crust wonder
bottle glass distorts a glance
— Maybe Buchan

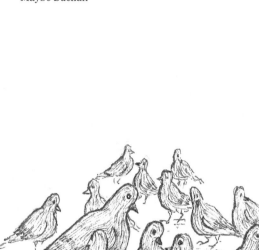

CORNER OF GRANVILLE AND BROADWAY

My eyes are new today, hollow,
empty, open and greedy for sights.
I claim this square of sidewalk
tight against the building,
where I am drinking coffee,
its surface patched with gum
scattered with salt crystals, cigarette butts
a feather, a corroded penny
and a green Starbucks stick plug,
my vision scoops like a loader filling
buckets brought to gather plunder.

The slabs are smoother at the edges,
the setter's trowel has formed a frame,
a stamp at one end reads 1988,
the outer section close to the road
is exposed aggregate,
it is stained in a line where rain
has dripped from the awning.
the cement is smoother and newer
as it curves around the corner
and follows the stream of vehicles
on this steamship of fat chance.

I dig in like a miner with gold fever,
rust streaks away from a socket
holding a traffic sign,
sun shines along the curb
and fans out across the blacktop,
like an arrow pointing out
the brighter side of the street,
pigeons skitter and flutter,
like emissaries, who wordlessly
warn the youth of salt crust wonder.

A sidewalk tree stands perky
next to a bicycle chained to a rack,
two post boxes and a *Metro* dispenser.
our children have come this way,
in shoes with lights and wheels,
they grow into Nikes and Fluvogs,
carry throw away coffee cups,
heads filled with life and times,
blind to the crack across the corner
and the myriad of ways that
bottle glass distorts a glance.

A WOMAN I KNEW

All her life she took on freight. Her mother trained her up, filling her little backpack with tomes citing the rules of engagement and tight packages of unremembered memories, then strapping it on with care — love — she called it.

She travelled well-worn tracks, stopping at endless stations, increasing her load. Sometimes she sped up, sliding past, head down, leaving the shipment on the platform. She felt guilty. Other times it took hours of tedium stuck in one place, while overflowing boxes were hefted aboard. Items foreign but familiar, were crammed into every empty space. Occasionally freight was unloaded and she became lighter for awhile.

It never lasted. There came a time when her bulging sides creaked and cracked. Moving forward became a greater and greater effort, she fell to her knees and then her belly. She cried and begged for help, wanting others to see the value of her cargo, to recognize the need and preciousness of what she carried. No one did, their eyes glazed over as they passed and turned their faces.

When it happened, she couldn't drag her self out of the way. A head-on hit, her cargo scattered, her body broken. She lost herself, in a maze of drips and gowns, unease lighting her edges. She was afraid she'd float away and dissipate like helium after a balloon burst. *Where is my freight, is it alright.* They brushed this aside. *Never mind that, just concentrate on healing yourself, take your time.*

They didn't understand the importance of regaining her rails. Only she could take the weight, knew each curve and incline like the veins in her arm. She left in the night, dragging her casts and bandages to the station. Placing her hands and knees into the familiar grooves, she moved forward.

Lost and desperate freight, hearing whispers of her return, stampeded. Claiming love, they didn't hear her cry out, but crushed her, sniffing, scratching and circling her carcass.

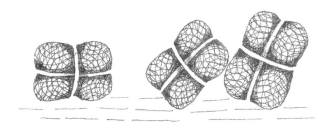

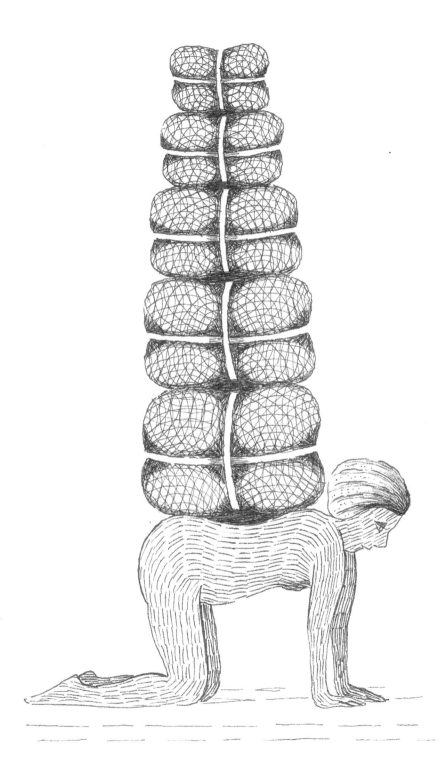

FREE RANGE

She was one of those women, heavy, filled with earth, her pelvis stretched out to cradle all who came within her orbit.

Plants flourished in her garden, purring into her fertilizing touch that gorged them into greater yields.

Her children were raised *free range*, like chickens, pecking into dusty corners for grubs and worms, with the sun, wind and rain working over them, teaching of heat and cold, dry and wet, their feet in constant contact with the soil — earth's porridge of minerals, bacteria and bits of narrative from other layers of time.

KEEP THE ODDS
EVEN

line up the cutlery
knives, forks and spoons
exact and even
across measured space
brush away crumbs
rub off the spots
leave no crack for demons
or excuse for the gods

by the light of a full moon
fold all the napkins
corner to corner
bleached and exact
crisp as egg shells
seams at a slant

rub the foot of a rabbit
half fill the glasses
keep water aligned
to a last equal drop

keep the odds even
steady the scales
cross all your fingers
avoid the black cat
polish the platters
spotless and gleaming
line down the center
five inches between

just make it perfect
with fine toothed
intention
don't be the cause
of our falling apart.

BROKEN PROMISE OF FLOWERS

In the fray of anemones,
the vendors snatch minutes
and fling an hour to bounce against
smells that mingle and pour
into the shrugs of aged wives,
their shoulders caved
from lack of bread, the fruit
of their orchards fermenting
in putrid heaps,
while old men spew a tirade,
claiming the bargain unfair,
when their backs were willow,
they had hoped for
— grander flowers —
what became of the orchids
and of the peonies?
what became of the bromeliads?
no one will console them
no one will descend into their
dementia and offer daffodils,
or carpets of pansies.
no one dares or cares
to bridge their swell of dismay
with blushing rosebuds.

A COAT OF PAINT

It was a promise she couldn't keep. Not with newborn eyes, and words that chewed her bowels hung out plainly like washing on a clothesline.

In a cocoon of rosy fog she'd bounced gleefully on a fluffy cloud of ignorance, smug with delight, glass clear and unchipped, their lives smooth as water — champagne and Chanel. All roads led to them. Travellers came and rested, munching tiny quiches on shaded lawns. They danced on the skin over an abscess, a coat of paint over dry rot, until the piston of clarity pierced the membrane.

— *Oh, to cap and seal it* — only for a day, or find a way to reweave a new basket with the thrashing strips. But knowing hardened inside her, tore away her flesh and magnified her heart. There was no juice, no meat to bend the truth. The wound was mortal the edges frayed and lifeless.

Just to be a child,
making piles of sand and mud
to house a princess,
when all the days were summer

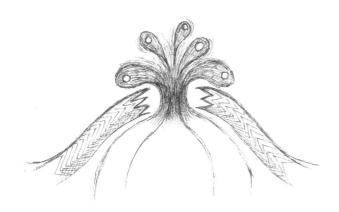

74

GOTHIC DREAM

I saw her
in her lime green dress
watching domino children fall,
apple cheeks, bright colours,
she blew them a kiss.
Their eyes followed
the masker,
hooded and scarlet.

A shovel of confetti cotton,
turned to bonbons in the crowd.
Burly figures circled,
looking for breaks
and shaking honey jars
to attract flies.

Flung on the floor
of a full flight carriage,
arms trapped,
lime green torn
and smeared and crushed,
She couldn't see the procession.

There was a sound
odd gibbering, lunar laughing,
that climbed and perched backwards
falling in sea lion coughs.
Searing sulphur breath,
so close.

I recollect the vehicle, weaving
gestures over cobble clouds,
shield raised to signify protection,
even as the driver disappeared
and burlap brutes banged fiery sticks
against the side.

The hands that pulled and rent her dress
reversed, returned, reshaped, caress.

VOYAGER

Gondola scenes
and wild wood falls,
dun doorjambs
and fortress walls.

In our bearded days,
when all was black and white,
we needed to be right.
undershirts were stuffed
with modern history,
a geography of delight
was buried alive, by
encyclopedic promises,
made during candle nights
of anxious lessons.

We spurred wild politics
to lathered exhaustion,
across smug atlas pages
covered in countries
with slip sliding borders.

Our shoes are dusty now
and all is shades of grey,
right has slid away.
wisdom erupts economically
fixing itself
to the sleeve of a tourist
standing near the dome.
What a waste, he says,
brushing it away.
it crawls across the plaza,
discarded edges limp,
delight ballooning
from it's center.

Journal covers
sigh content,
embrace companions
give consent,
sweet wanderlust
will turn to dust
and earth, but not relent.

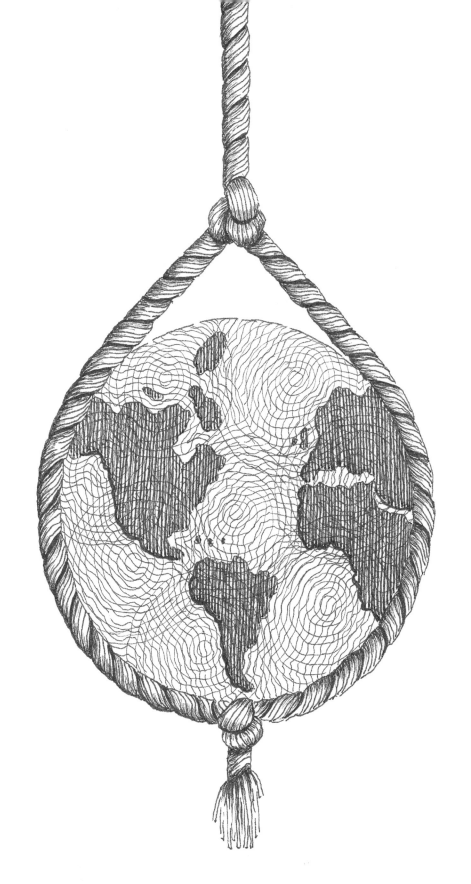

AQUA FAMILY

Curved dome sky,
frescoed by whisper images,
that curl and reshape,
turn back on themselves
in fluid re-formation.
a ghost bladder
gather, hold, release.

Drops pelt my face
trickle down my back
pool in my ears.
I feel the liquid of myself
slosh and gurgle,

as if ready to be
poured into varied containers,
a bucket for example,
a milk-bottle,
a vase, a jug

or spill across the floor,
mopped, wrung out
re-contained,

or ride ocean tides,
freeze into glaciers,
evaporate,
rain into puddles,
muddied and stuck
to boots and car tires,

carried into mingled
cohesion, a part
of the liquid world,

embraced and held
within an aqua-family,
that supports
whatever I become
and welcomes me
wherever I travel.

PHYLLIDA

She kept her English accent,
the economy of her speech
preserved it clear and bright,
for thirteen years after
the Empress of France
sailed with her small family,
from Liverpool to Montreal.
Her sister sandpapered the edges of *r*,
re-forged vowels
to Canadian shapes.
But the words of others
reached her in punctuated bites,
she bloomed in stilted motion,
her gathering and absorbing
elongated like a slug
crossing a dry path,
until days lost their footing,
spinning out
like gravel over a precipice,
and her accent hung
inexorably attached,
to the sweetened molecules
of her final breath.